The Art of Dining in Memphis

Joy Bateman
AUTHOR AND ILLUSTRATOR

Bon Appétit!
Joy Bateman

This book is dedicated to
my mother and father, Joyce and Lester Gingold

and

in memory of
my brother, Paul Meacham Gingold
and sister, Marion Slocum Fortas

ACKNOWLEDGMENTS

This book owes much to many people. My friend James R. Humphreys had confidence in the original concept and supported the project from the initial stages right up through final printing. Restaurant owners, chefs and other staff members patiently answered my questions and generously shared recipes. Thanks to all of you, many times over. I hope this book reflects admirably the wonderful dining experiences that were its inspiration.

Copyright © 2005
Joy Gingold Bateman

All rights reserved. No part of this book may be reproduced or transmitted in any form or by any means, electronic or mechanical, including photocopying, recording or by any information storage and retrieval system, without permission from the publisher.

Library of Congress Cataloging-in-Publication Data
ISBN 0-9773226-0-2

$21.95 plus S&H

Printed in the United States of America

Table of Contents

6 Anderton's
Eggplant Casserole
Deep Dish Apple Dumpling

8 Automatic Slim's Tonga Club
Goat Cheese Rellenos with Tomatillo Salsa

10 Azalea Grill
Trout Sautéed in Brown Butter with Golden Heirloom Tomatoes and Garlic
Roasted Beet Salad with Sage Goat Cheese, Toasted Walnuts and a Bacon-Shallot Vinaigrette

12 Bari Ristorante E Enoteca
Tonno con pomodoro e olive
Insalata di finocchio

14 The Blue Fish
The Blue Fish White Chocolate Bread Pudding, with Frozen Hazelnut Cream
Frozen Hazelnut Cream
Pan-Seared Diver's Scallops with Redeye Gravy

16 The Brushmark
Grilled Ahi Tuna Niçoise Salad
African Peanut Soup

18 Café 1912
Lyonnaise Salad

20 Café Society
Slow Cooked Salmon with Warm Salad of White Beans with Mustard and Sage
Pumpkin Soup

22 Capriccio Grill Italian Steakhouse
Chocolate Bread Pudding with cannoli cream

24 Chez Philippe
Rabbit with Sage Au Jus
Apple Cider Poached Mussels

26 Cielo
Blue Lump Crab Cakes with Avocado Velouté
Cocoa-dusted Escolar with Lemongrass Buerre Blanc

28 Equestria
Equestria Rockefeller Bisque

30 Erling Jensen's, the Restaurant
Praline Soufflé
Chocolate Soufflé

32 Felicia Suzanne's
Fried Green Tomatoes and Fresh Crab Salad with a drizzle of Balsamic Syrup

34 Folk's Folly
MM Medallions
Maker's Mark whiskey sauce
Fried Pickles

36 Ronnie Grisanti and Sons
Pasta Ala Elfo

38 The Grove Grill
Low Country Shrimp and Grits
Speckle Heart Grits

40 Jarrett's
Lobster Bisque with Brandied Crème Fraiche

42 Jim's Place East
Charcoaled Shish-ka-Bob

44 La Tourelle
La Tourelle Salad
Cassis Ice Cream

46 Lolo's Table
sautéed Red Snapper with Puttanesca
Wild Mushroom Bread Pudding

48 Lulu Grill
sautéed Red Snapper with Puttanesca
Carrot Cake

50 McEwen's On Monroe
Sweet Potato Encrusted Catfish
Green Corn pudding

52 paulette's
Yellow Squash Soup
Filet Paulette

54 Stella
Crawfish Cheesecake

56 Tsunami
Chilled Avocado Soup
Grand Marnier Soufflé

58 Wally Joe Restaurant
Grilled Loin of Lamb with Black Olive Crust, Celeriac-Potato Hash & Oven-Dried Tomato Red Wine Sauce

60 Woman's Exchange Tea Room
Seafood Bisque
Caramel Brownies
Brown Sugar Icing

62 Some Fare to be Recognized

63 Thoughts on Food

Dear Reader,

1959 PHOTO OF MY MOTHER AND ME IN FRONT OF NATIE'S, NEXT DOOR TO THE KNICKERBOCKER

My interest in dining started at an early age. I wasn't raised like normal Southern folk eating fried chicken and drinking Coke.
No black-eyed peas or turnip greens. At least not until I was in my teens.
The menu from the Memphis City Schools was my thing.
Good enough to make you sing.
A slice of fried bologna with a scoop of mashed potatoes with melted American cheese. And don't forget the little green peas.
The cooks in the kitchen were so nice. It didn't matter what they served, turnips, beets, beans or rice.
It was breakfast and often dinner too. Others didn't know, didn't have a clue.
At school I went back for seconds and thirds did the trick, never was I sick.
My mother couldn't keep food in the house.
Not to mislead you, it wasn't all bad. I'm not trying to make you sad.
My mother was unique, brilliant and in sync.

Every day we went to a restaurant called The Knickerbocker.
My brothers were busy playing sports, but never soccer.
When we were there, I wasn't always there to eat. However,
I always had a seat. It was my home away from home so I wouldn't be left alone.
I spent a lot of time talking to Tommy. Spoke of eggs, bagels and salami.
He was the chef behind the grill and wore a tall hat.
Said it wouldn't come off, that dirty rat.
Tommy was my friend and paid attention to me. He was kind and gave me tea.
When he wasn't flipping rib-eyes, T-Bones or New York Strips, we talked of boats, planes, and ships.

My father would go with us at night — he enjoyed every bite.
He had fried scallops on toast points and whipped mashed potatoes
sprinkled with paprika in circular rows. I shared his salad with Thousand Island dressing.
So delicious, so refreshing.

Years go by, on the fly, trying to keep from being shy. Tasting new cuisine at places I haven't seen .
In Boston, Legal Seafoods sets the mood. In Manhattan it was Sardi's and the Ocean Grill, both a thrill.
In Palm Beach, Petite Marmite could not compete, Hamburger Heaven, hot as hell.
In Chicago, spectacular seafood at Shaw's Crab House, the happening place,
I ordered so much, just in case.
San Francisco, fabulous Four-Star Fleur de Lys, and still quite good is Postrio.
Time to go — Home — To Memphis
Where we can catch a glimpse of the art of dining, without the rhyming.
Enjoy.
The Art Of Dining In Memphis.

Joy Bateman

Anderton's

1901 Madison Avenue • 901.726.4010

Since 1945, Anderton's has been a Memphis landmark and a big part of many people's lives. This old standby will no longer be standing after May of 2006. Anderton's retains its 1950's retro-style décor. Lighting is subdued, warm, and inviting. Known for great seafood and charcoal-broiled steaks. Lobster dainties are a specialty, and they are succulent, indeed. Anderton's apple dumpling recipe has a long history. Originating in the old Thompson's Cafeteria in downtown Memphis, the recipe was perfected by Robert Anderton's father in the 1940's. Best served piping hot with ice cream, the apple dumpling dessert is virtually a meal in itself. Anderton's, we will miss you!

EGGPLANT CASSEROLE

Peel and slice one large eggplant. Soak in cold salt water for one hour. Bread eggplant in cracker meal. Fry in canola oil until golden brown. Layer eggplant into a casserole dish. Pour two cans diced tomatoes over eggplant. Sprinkle one c sliced mushrooms, two tsp salt, two tsp pepper and one c Parmesan cheese over eggplant.

Bake at 350 degrees for 40 minutes.

Enjoy! Robert Anderton

DEEP DISH APPLE DUMPLINGS

3 c vegetable shortening
4 c flour
2 tsp salt

Mix well and let sit for 2 hours.

4 large apples, peeled and sliced
1 pound margarine
1/2 pound sugar
4 tbsp nutmeg

Bring to boil and cook for 20 minutes on low heat.

Roll dough. Using a 7 inch plate, cut 4 circles of piecrust. Fill each circle crust with drained apple mixture. Save liquid from apples. Pull crusts over the apple mixture to form a ball. Pinch crust together to seal. Place dumplings in a baking pan. Place sealed crust on bottom. Pour juice from the apples into the baking pan.

Bake at 375 degrees for 20 minutes or until dumplings are golden brown.

Automatic Slim's Tonga Club

83 S. Second • 525-7948

In 1986 Chef Karen Carrier opened Automatic Slim's in New York. In 1991, she opened Automatic Slim's in Memphis. Between Automatic Slims and her catering company, Another Roadside Attraction, Karen brought creativity to Memphis cuisine. Not one to rest on her laurels, she went on to establish Cielo, Beauty Shop, and Dō Sushi Restaurant. Chef Carrier has received local, national, and international recognition: she has put Memphis on the culinary map. At Automatic Slim's, the art exhibit changes every two months. Some of the featured artists have been Kristen Myers, Arline Jernigan, and Joel Hilgenburg. As for the food? Sensationally spicy. For lunch, the grilled cilantro lime chicken salad would be my choice, but the hottest selling item on the menu is jerk fish club. For dinner, Grill Chef Brown Burch's lamb chops with cardamom, nutmeg and sesame dust over sun-dried blueberry, jalapeño and mint chutney is impeccable, as is the coconut mango shrimp. Ask your server about the desserts. They are the best-kept secret, especially the strawberry cake. Shhhhh.

Goat Cheese Rellenos with Tomatillo Salsa

6 poblano chiles or Anaheim chiles
1 garlic clove — minced
1/4 pound goat cheese
1/4 pound Muenster cheese — grated
1 tbsp shallots — chopped
1/4 c cilantro — chopped
1/4 c basil — chopped
1 tbsp marjoram — chopped
1/4 tsp thyme — leaves pulled from the stem
1 egg
Salt and pepper to taste
1 tbsp heavy cream
Cornmeal for dredging
1/2 c peanut oil for sauté

Method: Roast & peel chiles. (Roast chiles on top of gas stove until charred all over & put into plastic ziplock bag for 15 minutes) Remove chiles from bag, carefully slicing one side & remove seeds, leaving stem intact. Set aside. Combine garlic, cheeses, shallots, basil, marjoram, thyme, salt and pepper. Pipe cheese mix into chiles. Do not overfill. Close chiles with toothpicks & refrigerate. Beat egg into cream & coat chiles carefully. Heat peanut oil in sauté pan over medium high heat. Dredge wet chile in cornmeal & sauté chiles. Remove chiles and set onto paper towel or brown bag to soak up oil. Remove toothpicks and serve immediately.

Tomatillo Salsa

15 tomatillos- husks removed, washed & charred
7 cloves of garlic — peeled
1 medium white onion — skin removed and quartered
3 serrano peppers — (judge by the taste as to whether you like it mild or hot & add accordingly) washed and stems removed
1-2 bunches of cilantro — washed and partial stems removed
Sugar to taste
Lime juice to taste
Salt and pepper to taste

Method: In a skillet over high heat or in a cast-iron skillet, place tomatillos till slightly charred and keep turning till charred on all sides. In a blender combine all ingredients, including tomatillos, except sugar, salt & pepper. Pulse till chunky but blended. Remove from blender and add sugar, salt & pepper to taste. To plate: Place rellenos in the middle of the plate and top with Tomatillo Salsa.

Azalea Grill

786 Echles • 901.452.0022

Azalea Grill, not at all lacking in charm, is nestled in the middle of the Normal Station neighborhood, close to the University of Memphis. Chef Linda Waller creates bountiful, innovative dishes for dinner, such as rack of lamb with roasted garlic in plum sauce, and pistachio-crusted sea bass with a sour cherry and Zinfandel glace. For lunch, she offers beautiful salads, homemade soups, and sandwiches such as grilled chicken with her famous Raspberry Chipotle Jam. Soft jazz piano music, live nightly. Dining on the patio in spring and fall is most delightful. As if the delicious food were not enough, wonderful aromas from the fresh herb and flower garden scent the air of the patio area lightly.

Trout Sautéed in Brown Butter with Golden Heirloom Tomatoes and Garlic

8 trout fillets
4 tbsp butter
Juice of 1 lemon
Salt and pepper to taste

3 golden tomatoes
8 whole peeled garlic cloves
1/2 large red onion, julienned
1/4 c olive oil
Splash of white wine
12 pitted kalamata olives
4 sprigs fresh basil

Cover garlic cloves with water and simmer 10-15 minutes till soft. Drain. Set aside.

To make the sauce; preheat oven to 500 degrees. Place tomatoes, garlic, onion in a roasting pan, uncovered. Drizzle with the olive oil. Toss. Splash on the wine and roast for approximately 20 minutes. Cover to keep warm and set aside.

Melt the butter in a sauté pan over low-med heat. Squeeze in lemon juice. As the butter begins to brown lightly, add trout fillets skin side up. Salt and pepper. Cook approximately 2 minutes. Flip and cook another 2 minutes. Plate 2 fillets per person. Top with roasted tomatoes. Garnish with pitted kalamata olives and a sprig of fresh basil.

Roasted Beet Salad with Sage Goat Cheese, Toasted Walnuts and a Bacon-Shallot vinaigrette

Serves 4
4 handfuls mesclun greens
4 medium size beets
6 heaping tbsp goat cheese
6-8 leaves fresh sage
Handful walnuts
1 tsp olive oil
1 tbsp brown sugar
For the vinaigrette:
4-6 slices cooked bacon
1 shallot, finely minced
1/2 tsp Dijon mustard
Herbes de Provence to taste
Salt to taste
2 tbsp red wine vinegar
1/2 c olive oil

Preheat oven to 500.
Clean beets and wrap in aluminum foil. Cook approximately 40 minutes or until tender. Peel back skin. Dice into large cubes. Set aside.
In a food processor combine cheese and sage. Set aside. In a sauté pan drizzle the walnuts with oil and sprinkle with brown sugar. Heat over medium high flame till sugar is melted. Set aside. Make the vinaigrette by whisking together all ingredients. To assemble, place greens on plate, top with the beets, then goat cheese and walnuts. Drizzle with vinaigrette. Serve.

Bari Ristorante E Enoteca

22 S. Cooper • 722-2244

Bari Ristorante e Enoteca recently underwent some major changes. What you see in this book is a view of Bari "before." Bari Ristorante has since doubled in size, and includes the "Enoteca," a very comfortable new bar and lounge. Chef Jason Severs' Southeastern Italian cuisine continues to be as delectable as ever. His sassy, serious bar menu offers twenty Italian cheeses, plus different kinds of antipasti, meats, olives, and frutti di mare. One can find limoncello here, when it doesn't seem too available anywhere else—such a nice Italian liqueur, quite pleasing to the palate at the end of a meal.

Tonno con pomodoro e olive
(Tuna with tomatoes and olives)

2 pounds fresh tuna, portioned into four steaks
16-20 cherry tomatoes, halved
30 good quality olives, pitted and halved
1/2 red onion, sliced thin
Chopped Italian parsley
Good quality extra virgin olive oil
Sea salt
Fresh ground pepper

Method: Prior to cooking the tuna, combine the tomatoes, olives, onions, a handful of parsley, about two tablespoons of olive oil, and salt and pepper, to taste. Mix just until ingredients are coated with olive oil, let stand for ten minutes. Grill the tuna to your desired temperature – we cook ours to rare at the restaurant. After cooking, cut the steaks on a bias, place a nice amount of the tomato mixture on top, drizzle with more extra virgin olive oil, serve. The most important part of this recipe is to have the flavors balance, i.e. if the onion is really strong, add less, same with the olives, etc.

Insalata di finocchio
(Fennel salad)
(This will serve four.)

2 bulbs of fresh fennel (the heavier the bulb is, the fresher it tends to be)
1/2 red onion
Juice of 10 oranges, cooked until the juice is reduced in half, then chilled
Good quality extra virgin olive oil
Chopped Italian parsley
Sea salt
Fresh ground black pepper

Method: Slice the fennel and onion very thinly. This can best be accomplished on a Japanese or French mandolin. Place in bowl with a little fresh parsley. Dress the salad with olive oil and orange juice reduction to taste, the same with the salt and pepper. Serve on a plate and garnish with fresh orange slices, and drizzle with more extra virgin olive oil to taste.

Blue Fish

2149 Young • 901.725.0230

Newcomers from Florida didn't leave anything behind. The fun, old Florida-style atmosphere and fresh seafood will transform your evening into a mini-vacation. A bit noisy, but not offensively so, considering the big picture. Fabulous, well-prepared dishes. The wine list offers many choices by the glass, and features Lolonis Winery of Mendocino County as the house wine. Lolonis wines are organic, by the way, as are all meats and free-range chicken served at The Blue Fish. Only at The Blue Fish would I kill for the appetizer, eggplant with jumbo lump crabmeat—crispy fried eggplant topped with crabmeat and a white butter sauce.

THE BLUE FISH WHITE CHOCOLATE BREAD PUDDING, WITH FROZEN HAZELNUT CREAM

1 13/9/2 baking dish, sprayed with non-stick oil spray
1 loaf white bread torn into chunks
4 large eggs
2 c heavy cream
1 c milk
2 1/2 c good quality white chocolate pieces, preferably Belgian or French
3/4 c hazelnut syrup or Frangelico liqueur

Preheat oven to 350 degrees, or 325 for convection. Pack bread chunks into pan, cover with white chocolate pieces. Blend eggs and cream well together. Drizzle milk around edges of pan. Drizzle hazelnut syrup over dry bread chunks. Pour egg mixture over entire pan. Bake covered with foil for 35 minutes, uncover and bake for 10 more minutes. Serve three scoops in a soup bowl, warmed, with a large scoop of Frozen Hazelnut Cream on top.

FROZEN HAZELNUT CREAM

Make this the night before you bake the pudding.

1 qt heavy cream
1 1/2 c hazelnut syrup
1 box confectioners sugar
Optional: chopped, toasted hazelnuts

In a mixer or food processor start blending cream and sugar, add syrup when it begins to thicken, add hazelnuts. Freeze overnight, or for at least six hours.

More options for bread puddings:
You can use leftover pound cake, muffins, croissants, in place of white bread.
You can leave off the hazelnut and add bananas and pecans and serve with vanilla ice cream or whipped cream. Let your imagination create your own style of bread pudding.

Note: You can use coffee flavoring syrups for the hazelnut, liqueurs, or organic flavoring extracts.

PAN-SEARED DIVER'S SCALLOPS WITH REDEYE GRAVY

2 large entrée portions

16 large, dry diver's scallops, 10/20 count, ask your fishmonger
1 c seasoned flour
2 fluid oz butter, clarified
1 c coffee
1/4 lemon, juice only
4 fluid oz demi-glace, gourmet food store brand
I pinch salt
2 servings mashed potatoes
1/4 bunch parsley, chopped fine

Heat butter in a large non-stick skillet on medium high heat. Dust scallops in seasoned flour and place in skillet. Sauté for 1 minute and turn over. Sauté 1 minute more and add coffee. Remove scallops to serving plate around mashed potatoes. Return pan to burner and add lemon juice, salt and demi-glace. Bring to boil and cook 1 minute. Remove from burner and pour over scallops and mashed potatoes. Garnish with parsley.

The Brushmark

1934 Poplar Avenue • 544.6225

Chef Penny McCraw combines her passions for the arts and food to create her own style of New American cuisine. The Brushmark, located inside Brooks Museum, is a treasure not to be missed. Panoramic windows lead from the indoor dining area to the terrace, which offers a breathtaking view of historic Overton Park. Lunch is served daily, except Mondays. Lunch menu selections include fried chicken cobb salad, spinach and strawberry salad, and hot ham and cheddar sandwiches. On the first Wednesday of each month, when the Museum hosts special theme events, The Brushmark also serves dinner. Ten percent discount given to Brooks Museum members.

GRILLED AHI TUNA NIÇOISE SALAD

Makes 6 servings

NIÇOISE SALAD DRESSING

1/4 c red wine vinegar
1 large garlic clove minced and mashed to a paste with 1/4 tsp of salt
1 1/2 tsp minced shallots
2 tbsp plus 1 tsp Dijon mustard
2 c blended oil
Kosher salt and fresh black pepper

In medium bowl, whisk together vinegar, garlic, shallots and mustard. Slowly whisk in the oil to emulsify. Season to taste with salt and pepper. You can refrigerate in a covered container for 1 week.

SALAD

3/4 pound haricots verts, trimmed
1 1/2 pounds small Yukon Gold potatoes
6 4oz ahi tuna steaks (at least 1 inch thick)
1 1/2 oz drained bottled capers
3/4 pounds baby mixed greens
Olive oil
1 pt grape tomatoes
2/3 c pitted Niçoise olives
4 large hard-boiled eggs, quartered
3 tablespoons chopped fresh parsley and basil

Trim the haricots verts, then blanch in salted boiling water 3 to 4 minutes. Immediately transfer to ice bath to stop cooking. Add potatoes to boiling water and simmer, until tender, 15 to 20 minutes, then drain. Halve potatoes while still warm and toss with 2 tablespoons dressing, then cool.

Brush tuna with olive oil and season with salt and pepper. Grill over moderately high heat for 2 to 3 minutes on each side, keeping the centers rare. Remove from heat and slice each steak. Drizzle with 2-3 tablespoons of dressing and top with capers.

To serve, divide the haricots verts, potatoes, tomatoes, eggs and olives into 6 portions. For each plate, arrange each ingredient by placing them in a clockwise fashion around the rim of plate. Toss the greens with 2-3 tablespoons of dressing and mound in middle of plate. Arrange the tuna on sides of salad. Sprinkle with chopped parsley and basil.

AFRICAN PEANUT SOUP

1 tbsp vegetable oil
1 garlic clove, chopped
2 c stewed tomatoes
1 chopped yellow bell pepper
1 chopped onion
1 chopped red bell pepper
1 chopped green bell pepper
1 c extra crunchy peanut butter
6 c chicken broth
2 chicken breasts, grilled and diced
Red chili flakes to taste

Sauté vegetables in oil until wilted. Add remaining ingredients, stirring well to incorporate. Cook over medium-low heat for 30 minutes. Adjust seasoning with salt, pepper, and chili flakes.

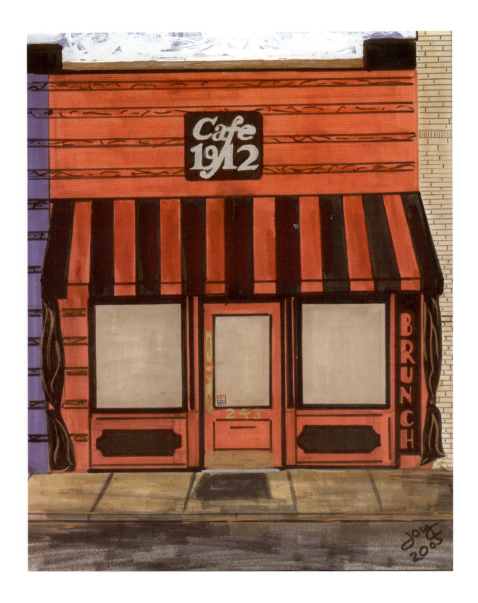

Café 1912

243 S. Cooper • 722.7200

This lively, cozy bistro is usually bustling. The open kitchen gives a warm and friendly welcome to diners. Not pretentious. Café 1912 specializes in French/Continental cuisine. Many delicious choices to please everyone. Among the varied menu items: oysters Rockefeller, muffuletta, poached salmon, guava pepper barbecue shrimp, deep-fried catfish, roasted pork tenderloin, and niçoise salad with fresh tuna, potatoes, olives and hard-boiled eggs. Since Café 1912 stays open a little later than many other restaurants, diners can stop for a meal after the theater, movies or sporting events. Moderately priced. Good selection of wines, none more than five dollars per glass.

Lyonnaise Salad

1/2 pound small potatoes in their skin
1/4 pound petite green beans
2 ripe tomatoes, sliced or cut in wedges
4 slices of bacon, cooked
3/4 - 1 c vinaigrette
Spring mix salad greens
4 eggs — poached or soft-boiled (Do this last.)

Cook the potatoes in their skins. Remove when slightly firm, peel and dice.
Blanche the beans in boiling salted water until they are cooked but still slightly firm.
Place the greens in a large bowl with the vinaigrette and mix. Arrange the greens on 4 large plates. Add the beans and potatoes to the vinaigrette left in the bowl and coat. Arrange them on the greens. Place tomatoes on each salad. Garnish each with a bacon slice. Place one egg on each salad. (See below.) Drizzle with any leftover vinaigrette.
(Anchovies may be added if you like.)

Eggs: At Café 1912, we poach the eggs in boiling water and then place one on each salad. You may also boil the eggs for 4 minutes, cool and carefully shell them, and immediately place them on the salad.

Café Society

212 S. Evergreen • 722.2177

Café Society, specializing in Continental cuisine, has always been reliable for romantic atmosphere, delicious food, and friendly staff, but now they have raised the bar. Café owner, Chef Michel Leny, a native of Belgium, comes to fine cuisine naturally—his father was a chef at world famous Maxim's, in Paris. Café Society's expanded dining area is something to see. Smartly decorated and classy, with vibrant paintings by local artists. Chef Cullen Kent, new to the staff, is an awesome chef who pays close attention to detail. Of the numerous items he has added to the menu, here are but a few: celery rémoulade with poached egg and shrimp; petite tartlets of pan-seared sea scallops with leeks, turnips, brie and verjus beurre blanc; and confit leg of duck, served with warm green lentils in vinaigrette. Conveniently located in Midtown, Café Society is a great place to meet clients for lunch. And, too, a great date place. Bon appétit!

SLOW COOKED SALMON WITH WARM SALAD OF WHITE BEANS WITH MUSTARD AND SAGE

4-6 oz pieces of salmon
1/2 pound dried white beans
1 onion
1 stalk celery
1 carrot
1 bunch sage
1 1/2 tbsp mustard
2 shallots
Olive oil
Lemon juice
Salt and pepper

Coat salmon in olive oil, season with salt and pepper, and place in 200 degree oven for 15 minutes. Soak beans overnight and cook with mirepoix and 1/2 bunch sage. When beans are done, drain and add fresh chopped sage, mustard and lemon juice. Season and serve salmon over beans and drizzle with olive oil.

PUMPKIN SOUP

(serves 10 – freezes well)

2 French green pumpkins (available at Asian markets) peeled and seeded
1 stalk celery
1 onion, diced
4 shallots
4 cloves garlic
1 orange zest and juice
Vegetable stock to cover
Salt and pepper
1/2 pound butter

Combine ingredients and cook until pumpkin is done. Puree and add back to pot. Whisk in butter and adjust seasoning. Serve with shellfish garnish or as a sauce for shellfish.

Capriccio Grill Italian Steakhouse

149 Union Avenue • 529.4199

When I am busy, I don't always know what day it is. Thank goodness Capriccio Grill Italian Steakhouse is open seven days a week, always serving something really good, at just about all hours. Located inside the Peabody Hotel. Attractive and friendly staff. This is a dependable, top-flight restaurant. The steaks here are cooked to perfection. So is the asparagus. "The Wedge" is an excellent choice for a very nice, simple salad. With many different pasta dishes and pizzas to choose from, diners have a taste of Italy at their fingertips.

Chocolate Bread Pudding with Cannoli Cream

1 tsp unsalted butter
2 c heavy cream
2 c semisweet chocolate chips
4 eggs
1 c light brown sugar
1/4 c Grand Marnier
8 slices brioche or egg-based bread
1 c golden raisins
1 tbsp vanilla

1. Preheat oven to 350 degrees.
2. grease a 9 1/4 by 5 1/4 by 2 1/2 inch loaf pan with butter
3. In a large sauce pan heat cream to a simmer with vanilla.
4. Mix in a large bowl sugar, eggs, Grand Marnier
5. Cube bread and place off to the side.
6. Once cream comes to a simmer pour over chocolate chips, whisk till combined.
7. Temper one ladle of the chocolate mix into the egg mixture.
8. Slowly incorporate the rest.
9. Toss in bread and mix till coated.
10. Pour into baking pan and let rest for 30 minutes.
11. Top with 1 c chocolate chips.
12. Bake for 55 minutes covered or until center has set like custard.

Cannoli Cream

2 c ricotta impastata
1 c powdered sugar
1/8 c Galliano cordial

1. In a mixer whip ricotta till smooth, about 5 minutes.
2. Add powdered sugar and Galliano and whisk till fully incorporated.

Chez Philippe

149 Union Avenue • 529.4188

What can be more elegant than sitting on the couch at a table in the dining room at Chez Philippe, listening to soft, lovely, delightful music? The décor is rich and lavish. Glittering mirrored crystal chandeliers throughout; gorgeous gold leaf faux finishes used generously on painted surfaces. Former Chez Philippe Master Chef Jose Gutierrez set the gold standard for fine dining in Memphis in years past. Chef Gutierrez is now gone, but the staff has successfully carried on in his grand tradition of excellence. The only Mobil Four-Star Restaurant in the Mid South, Chez Philippe is as wonderful as ever. My hot lobster bisque with vichyssoise martini and shaved truffles, and my entrée of four-hour braised beef short ribs, served with cauliflower risotto and vegetables julienne, were magnificent. Menu selections are well priced. As of this writing, Chez Philippe's style of cuisine is set to change from classic French, to French with an Asian flair. Closed Sunday and Monday.

RABBIT WITH SAGE AU JUS

4 whole rabbits
2 bottles(750 ml) red wine
1 qt demi-glace
2 c sage leaf
4 c celery (chopped)
4 c carrots (chopped)
4 c onion (chopped)
1 -2 tbsp garlic (chopped)
2 oz unsalted butter

Clean rabbits. In a large roasting pan, add olive oil and heat on stove at medium. Add rabbits to pan and cook until brown. Deglaze with red wine and reduce for 2 – 3 minutes. Add chopped onions, celery and carrots. Cook on stove for 5 minutes. When vegetables are almost done, remove rabbits and add salt, pepper and butter. Reduce for another 5 minutes.
Serves 8 people, half a rabbit each.

APPLE CIDER POACHED MUSSELS

2 c white wine
1 pound New Zealand mussels
1/4 c apple cider
1 tbsp salt
1/4 tsp black pepper
1 1/2 c heavy cream
3 tbsp tomato paste

Clean mussels, taking off any beards. Do not use any mussels that are not closed. (If mussels are open, tap on them to get them to close. If they still do not close, do not use.) Cook mussels in white wine and cider until they open (remove any mussels that don't open and throw out). Add salt, pepper, heavy cream and tomato paste. Bring to simmer. Remove mussels. Strain liquid through a China Cap or coffee filter. Place mussels in a serving bowl and pour strained liquid on top. Season to taste.

Cielo

679 Adams • 524.1886

ot the trendy restaurant you might be expecting, Cielo is in a class by itself. Exceptionally original. So NOT Memphis! The ambience is romantic and elegant. Having the well-known, talented Di Anne Price at the piano every Friday and Saturday night is a strong draw. I am sold on Chef David Scott Lorrison's French Fusion cuisine. After trying the braised sea scallops with warm Camembert and port reduction, I recall the taste, and my mouth still waters. The grilled beef tenderloin stuffed with sage Derby, served with roasted roma demi-glace and pommes frites is worth serious consideration. Nightly specials. Cielo is located in the historic Victorian Village area.

BLUE LUMP CRAB CAKES WITH AVOCADO VELOUTÉ

BLUE CRAB CAKES

This will yield 8 servings.

1 pound lump crab
1/2 c seeded diced tomatoes
1/2 c chopped scallions
1 heaping tsp of whole grain Dijon mustard
3/4 c Japanese bread crumbs (Panko — available at local Asian markets / Toasted bread crumbs may be substituted.)
3 whole eggs
1/4 c heavy cream
Pinch of salt and white pepper

Mix all the ingredients thoroughly in a mixing bowl. Heat a teaspoon of butter in a non-stick pan until golden brown. Spoon a large dollop of crab mixture into the pan and turn in two minutes. Remove when golden brown. Place in 450 degree oven for 3-4 minutes until firm.

AVOCADO VELOUTÉ:

1 semi-soft avocado, peeled and seeded
2 c chicken bouillon or stock
 (Canned broth will work.)

Place the avocado and bouillon in a small pot on the stove and bring to a light simmer. Immediately remove from heat and purée in blender and season with salt and white pepper. Keep sauce at room temperature.

To serve: Place two crab cakes on each serving plate and spoon Avocado Velouté on and around cakes.

COCOA-DUSTED ESCOLAR WITH LEMONGRASS BUERRE BLANC

6 oz escolar
Olive oil
Salt and pepper to taste
3 tbsp butter (unsalted)
Cocoa powder for dusting

Coat escolar in olive oil, salt and pepper, then coat in cocoa powder. Sear in butter and finish in the oven for 8 minutes.

LEMONGRASS BUERRE BLANC

1 c dry vermouth
Pinch of saffron
1 stem lemongrass roughly chopped
1 tsp shallots, minced
1/8 c white wine vinegar
1/4 c heavy cream
1/2 pound of butter (softened)
Salt and white pepper to taste

Combine all ingredients and reduce by two thirds. Add 1/4 c cream and reduce till thick. Whisk in 1/2 pound of soft butter. Strain liquid and add salt and white pepper to taste. Plating for service: Put Buerre Blanc in the middle of the plate and place Cocoa-Dusted Escolar on top.

 Equestria

3165 Forest Hill Irene Road • Germantown • 869.2663

There are just a few restaurants of Equestria's caliber in the suburbs of Memphis. With higher fuel prices, Equestria's location in the Germantown area could be a real plus for those who live out in that direction and are looking for great food close to home. For those who live closer to downtown Memphis, the drive out to Equestria is well worth the trip. Equestria offers International New Vogue Fusion cuisine. One interesting menu choice is oven-dried, crusted Tilapia, served with saffron whipped potatoes, grilled asparagus and balsamic raspberry vinaigrette. Another temptation would be the Niman Ranch pork rib rack with grilled Fayette County peaches, grain mustard spaetzle and peach demi-glace. The lobster and shrimp avocado salad showcases the culinary talent of Chef Kevin Rains: seafood and avocado are tossed with Russian fingerling potatoes, roasted baby beets, applewood bacon and lemon grass vinaigrette. This hearty appetizer could serve as a meal, and it tastes as spectacular as it looks. Owners strive to make your dining experience memorable. Menu changes bimonthly.

EQUESTRIA ROCKEFELLER BISQUE

Chef Kevin Rains
Serves six

1 pound fresh de-stemmed spinach
1/2 c coarsely chopped onion
1/2 c chopped celery with leaves
1/4 chopped green onions
1/4 c fresh chopped parsley
1/2 c coarsely chopped iceberg lettuce
1/2 c (1 stick) butter
2 tbsp anchovy paste
1/2 tsp Greek seasoning
1/2 tsp freshly ground black pepper
2 tbsp fresh lemon juice
3 tbsp flour
2 c chicken broth
2 tsp Worcestershire
1/4 tsp soy sauce
1 pt small oysters, 1/2 c liquid reserved
2 c half-and-half
2 tbsp freshly grated Parmesan cheese
2 tbsp sambuca or anise-flavored liqueur
dash cayenne

Garnish:
3 tbsp toasted bread crumbs

Preparation:
In food processor, purée spinach, onion, celery, green onions, parsley and lettuce. In large stockpot, melt butter over low heat. Add spinach mixture and cook ten minutes, stirring frequently. Add anchovy paste, Greek seasoning, pepper and lemon juice. Whisk in flour and cook three minutes. Gradually add chicken broth, Worcestershire, soy sauce and cayenne. Heat to boiling over medium-high heat. Reduce heat to low and simmer five minutes.

Just before serving, add oysters with liquid, over low heat, and simmer another two minutes. Add half-and-half, Parmesan and liqueur and continue to simmer until thoroughly heated. DO NOT BOIL. Garnish with toasted bread crumbs.

Erling Jensen, The Restaurant

1044 S. Yates • 763.3700

Erling Jensen, The Restaurant, continues to be at the top of my list. Where else is the staff so gracious and kind? Where else does one find amusettes of avocado, pineapple and tuna ceviche? White linen tablecloths and gorgeous fresh flowers on every table? Chef Erling Jensen is known for his globally inspired, classically executed cuisine, featuring the freshest seasonal ingredients: fine dining of the highest caliber. The rack of lamb with pecan, mustard, garlic and molasses crust is melt-in-your-mouth divine. Portions are amazingly large. At my table, I sampled the halibut with jumbo lump crabmeat and truffle leek cream. Superb! This lovely, sophisticated, elegant, intimate restaurant ROCKS!

Praline

Preheat the oven to 350. Warm 1 1/3 c sliced almonds in the oven for ten minutes. Meanwhile, melt 3/4 c of sugar in a saucepan with a splash of water until clear, stirring once or twice. Add a squeeze of lemon juice, then raise the heat and cook to a light caramel color. Stir in the almonds then pour onto a flat parchment lined baking sheet. Allow to cool, then crush praline with a rolling pin.

Praline Soufflé
(makes 12 ramekins)

2 c whole milk
1 c superfine sugar
1 quantity praline
1/2 c all purpose flour
8 large eggs, 4 separated
Pan spray or butter for ramekins

First make the base mix with all of the milk and 1/2 of the sugar and all but 1/2 c of the praline. Beat together the flour, 4 whole eggs and 4 yolks. Gradually whisk in the praline mixture, then return to the heat and simmer until the mixture is very thick and smooth. Cool mixture.

Place the 4 egg whites in the bowl of an electric mixer with a pinch of salt. Begin to whip the whites until they are thick and glossy. Gradually add the sugar and allow to whip to medium peaks.

While waiting for the meringue to whip, sugar the ramekins and dust with the remaining praline.

Fold the meringue into the base mixture and fill the ramekins with the soufflé mixture. Bake at 350 for about 15 to 20 minutes

Chocolate Soufflé
(makes 12 ramekins)

9 eggs, separated
18 oz semisweet chocolate
8 oz butter
1 c sugar

In the bowl of an electric mixer add the egg whites with a pinch of salt and begin mixing. Allow the meringue to rise before you slowly and gradually add the sugar. Put the butter and chocolate together in a bowl and melt over simmering water. When melted, remove from the heat and add the egg yolks and incorporate. When the meringue reaches medium stiff peaks, stop the machine. Then gently fold the meringue and chocolate together and pipe into soufflé dishes. Bake at 350 for 20 to 25 minutes.

Felicia Suzanne's

80 Monroe • 523.0877

Chef *Felicia Willett captures the true fine dining experience at Felicia Suzanne's. Casually elegant, with open space, Felicia Suzanne's offers exquisite American cuisine with contemporary Southern influences. Having spent seven years working with internationally acclaimed Chef Emeril Lagasse in New Orleans, Felicia is anything but green. Chef Emeril taught her what most could not learn in a lifetime. Hence the strong New Orleans influence, which is especially poignant at this time. A few selections to whet your appetite are the classic Creole turtle soup, shrimp and grits, bone-in double-cut veal chops and crispy Louisiana oysters tossed in a New Orleans barbecue sauce. The salad of baby mixed greens with crumbled Maytag blue cheese, spiced walnuts and dried cherries tossed in walnut oil, with a drizzle of balsamic syrup and a homemade cheese straw, is out of this world. Memphis is proud to have Felicia Suzanne's in downtown Memphis.*

FRIED GREEN TOMATOES AND FRESH CRAB SALAD WITH A DRIZZLE OF BALSAMIC SYRUP

2 c balsamic vinegar
1/2 c light brown sugar
Couple of sprigs of fresh thyme
Pinch of black pepper
12 slices of fresh green tomatoes, cut 1/2 inch thick
Salt and freshly ground black pepper
1 c flour
2 eggs, beaten with 2 tablespoons milk
2 c fine dried breadcrumbs
2 c vegetable oil
1 c mayonnaise
1 tbsp Creole mustard
1/4 c chopped fresh tarragon leaves
1/4 c capers, finely chopped
2 tbsp finely chopped fresh parsley leaves
2 hard boiled eggs, grated
Crystal Hot Sauce

1 pound fresh domestic lump crabmeat, picked for cartilage

In a non-reactive saucepan, over medium heat, combine the vinegar, sugar, thyme and black pepper. Bring to a boil and cook until the mixture becomes thick and syrupy, about 8 minutes. Remove from the heat and strain. Cool completely. Season both sides of the tomatoes with salt and pepper. Allow to sit for 10 minutes. Add the flour, egg wash and breadcrumbs in three separate shallow pans. Season each mixture with salt and pepper. Dredge each tomato in the seasoned flour, coating completely. Dip each tomato in the egg wash, letting the excess drip off. Finally dredge in the seasoned breadcrumbs, coating completely. In a large sauté pan, over medium heat, add the oil. When the oil is hot, fry the tomatoes until crispy, about 2 minutes. Turn the tomatoes over and continue to cook. Remove and drain on paper towels. Season with salt and pepper. In a mixing bowl, combine the mayonnaise, mustard, tarragon, capers, parsley and eggs. Mix well. Season with salt and Crystal Hot Sauce. Fold in crabmeat.

To serve, place a fried tomato in the center of each plate. Spoon some of the crab salad over the tomatoes. Top the salad with another tomato, pressing the tomato slightly, forming a sandwich. Drizzle the entire plate with some of syrup.

Yields: 6 servings
Recipe courtesy of Felicia Willett, 2003

Folk's Folly

551 S. Mendenhall • 762.8200

Folk's Folly Prime Steak House & Prime Cut Shoppe, established in 1977, has been named one of "America's Top Ten Steak Houses" by the International Restaurant and Hospitality Rating Bureau. In virtually every restaurant poll, Memphians choose Folk's Folly as THE place to go for the best steak in town. Wine connoisseurs rejoice over the selection of four hundred fine wines. Wine Spectator has recognized Folk's Folly with its "Award of Excellence" since 1999, and has noted the hearty portions and outstanding service diners can expect. In addition to the obvious choices which we all relish—-the filet mignon, the New York strip and the rib eye—-Folk's Folly offers us the Scottish salmon fillet. The she-crab soup is not to be missed, unless you are on a diet. So rich and creamy and laced with sherry. Folk's Folly has always been a favorite place to entertain clients. Reservations recommended.

MM Medallions

2- 4 to 5 oz tenderloin medallions
Season with cracked black pepper
Grill to desired temperature.
Place 4 oz of MM sauce on a warm plate with full coverage. Place medallions in center of plate and garnish with parsley.

Maker's Mark Whiskey Sauce

yield 1/2 gallon

1/3 pound fresh shallots
5 oz Maker's Mark whiskey
1 1/2 oz drawn butter
2 1/2 oz minced garlic
3 1/4 c au jus
3 1/4 c chicken stock
4 3/4 c heavy cream
2 tbsp fresh lemon juice
1 tsp cornstarch
2 tsp cracked black pepper
2 tsp green peppercorns

Blend shallots and whiskey together in a food processor. Strain shallots and reserve whiskey. Sauté strained shallots and garlic in butter until tender. Add whiskey to deglaze pan. On high heat, add stock and au jus, reducing down to 1 1/2 c, approximately 1 hour. Add cream and bring to a simmer. Mix cornstarch and lemon juice together. Stir in slowly. When sauce has slightly thickened, remove from heat and add pepper and peppercorns. Serve immediately.

Fried Pickles

Yield 8 servings

2 eggs
2 3/4 c milk
3 c flour
2 tsp baking powder
2 tsp Lawry's Seasoned Salt
1/2 tbsp salt
1/2 tbsp white pepper
1/2 gallon dill pickles, peeled and sliced

In a large mixing bowl beat eggs. Add all ingredients mixing to a medium thickness. Dip pickles in batter and deep fry. Serve immediately.

Ronnie Grisanti and Sons

2855 Poplar Avenue • 323.0007

Where Memphians go for upscale, authentic Italian fare is a no-brainer. Yes, Ronnie Grisanti and Sons Restaurant! Specializing in homemade Tuscan cuisine, offering manicotti, ravioli, and Marsala medallions of veal. A perennial favorite on the menu is the pan-seared Chilean sea bass over a bed of risotto, with shiitake mushrooms, roma tomatoes and artichoke hearts, topped with white wine thyme sauce. Simply divine. The Grisanti family came to Memphis from Valdottavo, Italy, in 1903, and opened their first restaurant. In 1978, Ronnie Grisanti and Sons opened in the original Sun Studio location. Now in a newer location on Poplar, the restaurant proudly serves not only locals, but visiting celebrities like Morgan Freeman, George Hamilton and Marlo Thomas. Ronnie Grisanti and Sons is open Monday through Saturday for dinner.

Pasta Ala Elfo

Serves 2
Buttered Spaghetti with Shrimp and Mushrooms

Thin spaghetti
Salt
Pepper
Butter
Garlic
Jumbo shrimp
Mushrooms
Romano cheese
Olive Oil

Spaghetti

Cook 4 ounces of thin spaghetti with 2 tablespoons of olive oil in rapidly boiling water for 10 minutes. ("Use long fork to stir spaghetti so it won't wed," were the chef's romantic directions.) Drain, rinse with cold water, peel and set aside.
Heat in a large skillet: 2 c butter.
Add 6 large cloves of garlic, minced, 6 jumbo raw shrimp, quartered, and 4 large mushrooms, thinly sliced. Cook in the hot butter for 5 minutes. Sprinkle with 4 tablespoons freshly grated Romano cheese and freshly ground white pepper. Using a large spoon, turn spaghetti over from edge of skillet to center, being careful not to cut it. Don't stop tossing. Continue until spaghetti is very hot, but do not let the butter brown. When cooking this dish it is important to know that the heat is increased progressively going from low to medium to hot. Turn out onto warm serving dish and serve with freshly grated Romano cheese and freshly chopped parsley.

The Grove Grill

4550 Poplar Avenue • 818.9951

Moving from the Upper East Side of New York to yuppie territory in the heart of East Memphis, restaurateur Chip Apperson opened The Grove Grill along with his friend and Culinary Institute of America classmate, Jeffrey Dunham, in 1997. I think anyone would agree that the two CIA grads have done an excellent job, and that The Grove Grill is here to stay. This American bistro has an extensive menu, which includes a plethora of vegetables. I particularly like the warm blue cheese slaw and the praline sweet potatoes. Some popular entrees are drunken pork tenderloin, seafood pasta jambalaya and rotisserie chicken. The dining area feels relaxed, yet refined, and with its ever-changing art exhibit, is most attractive.

Low Country Shrimp and Grits

2 pounds shrimp, peeled (16 to 20 count per pound)
4 tsp Cajun seasoning
4 tbsp vegetable oil
4 tbsp minced garlic
4 oz diced tasso ham
4 tbsp chopped fresh herbs (parsley, thyme, rosemary and basil)
4 oz dry white wine
8 oz shrimp stock
4 tbsp whole butter
4 tbsp chopped scallions
Salt to taste
1 recipe speckle heart grits (recipe follows)

Preheat a large skillet to medium-high heat. Toss shrimp in Cajun spice. Add oil to skillet. Add garlic, tasso and shrimp to pan. Sauté for 2 to 3 minutes, add herbs and wine. Cook for an additional 1 or 2 minutes. Add shrimp stock and bring to a boil. Portion grits into 4 to 6 large bowls and place equal portions of shrimp into each bowl on top of the grits. Return pan to heat and bring to a simmer. Reduce by up to 1/2 volume, remove from heat and whisk in whole butter. Pour sauce evenly over the top of each bowl of shrimp and grits. Garnish with chopped scallions. Serves 8.

Speckle Heart Grits

3 c chicken stock
2 c milk
1/4 c whole butter
1 c stone ground grits
Salt to taste
Tabasco sauce to taste

Combine 2 c stock (reserve 1 c stock), milk and butter in a double boiler and bring to a simmer. Add grits while stirring constantly for 5 minutes. Place in a double boiler and cook for 1 to 2 hours, stirring occasionally. Add additional stock while cooking to adjust to desired consistency. Season with salt and Tabasco sauce to taste (take care not to over salt). Serves 4 to 6.
Prepared by Chef Jeffrey Dunham.

Jarrett's

5689 Quince Road • 763.2264

Jarrett's Chef Rick Farmer became interested in the culinary arts early in life. While working at big-name restaurants in New York, he prepared food for celebrities like Barbara Walters, Eddie Murphy and Stevie Wonder. From New York, he moved to Biarritz, where he worked alongside two other chefs at Restaurant Marcot. Here he encountered Basque cuisine, in which seafood plays a central role, and which shows traces of both Spanish and French traditions. Basque cooking influences Chef Farmer's cooking style today. Only the very freshest fish and shellfish are served. This emphasis on high quality fish and shellfish may account in part for the excellence of Jarrett's Regional American cuisine. The horseradish-crusted grouper on garlic mashed potatoes is a winner by far.

Lobster Bisque with Brandied Crème Fraiche

3 qts lobster stock
1/2 4 oz can roasted red peppers (pureed)
1 pinch saffron
1 tbsp garlic
White roux (1/2 pound butter and 1/2 pound flour)
1/2 large cooking spoon tomato paste
1/2 tsp cayenne pepper
1 tbsp paprika
1/2 qt cream
1/2 qt milk
1 oz brandy
4 oz cooked and chopped lobster meat from claw joints
4 oz cooked and chopped shrimp

Combine lobster stock, roasted red peppers, saffron and garlic and bring to a boil. Add the tomato paste, cayenne pepper and paprika. Whisk in blond roux to achieve soup consistency and add milk and cream. Season with salt and pepper and add brandy. Garnish with lobster meat, shrimp and brandied crème fraiche.

Brandied crème fraiche

1 c crème fraiche
1/2 oz brandy
1/8 tsp allspice
1/3 tsp coriander
1/3 tsp cinnamon

Whisk all ingredients together to form soft peaks.

Lobster stock

1 oz olive oil (extra virgin)
Shells and heads from 4 cooked lobsters (crushed with a meat mallet)
1 large carrot (sliced thin)
1 medium onion (sliced thin)
2 stalks celery (sliced thin)
Zest from 1 orange
6 or 7 cloves of garlic
1 sprig fresh tarragon
1 sprig fresh thyme
2 bay leaves
1 pinch saffron
1/2 bottle white wine
3 qts cold water

Heat the olive oil in a large roasting pan until smoking hot. Add lobster shells and heads and cook for a few minutes. Add all the remaining ingredients except the wine and the water and cook for another 6-7 minutes or until the vegetables are beginning to soften. Add the wine and water and simmer for 30 minutes. (Begin timing when the stock begins to simmer.)

Jim's Place East

5560 Shelby Oaks Drive • 388.7200

An old Memphis favorite that's off the beaten trail is not to be forgotten. Surrounded by glorious oak trees, tulip poplars, and magnolias in a park-like setting. "A Memphis Landmark in Fine Dining" since 1921. Authentic Greek and Southern cuisine with such specialties as souflima, mousaka, chicken spanakotpita, and last, but not least, baklava for dessert. Jim's Place is also known for excellent charcoal-broiled steaks, The grilled calf's liver is remarkably good. The asparagus mousse, created by owner Tina Taras Liollio, has kept a low profile — it deserves applause with a standing ovation. Slightly sweet, light and refreshing. Jim's Place is elegant and quite comfortable. Definitely a keeper.

CHARCOALED SHISH-KA-BOB

Yield: 8 servings

2 pounds lamb or beef
3 cloves garlic, minced
1/4 c Burgundy wine
1/2 c salad oil
2 tsp oregano
2 onions
2 bell or red peppers
16 fresh mushrooms
Salt and pepper to taste

Marinade
Juice of 4 lemons
1/2 tsp oregano
1/4 c salad oil

Cut meat into 1-1 1/2" cubes

Place meat in large plastic or stainless steel bowl and add garlic, oil, wine, salt, pepper and oregano and mix well.

Quarter onions, cube peppers.

Skewer meat alternating it with onions and peppers. Add mushroom to each end.

Charcoal over hot coals or broil in oven to desired doneness.

Baste with lemon oil marinade after you remove from grill.

CREMA KARAMELA

Caramel Custard

Temperature 350º
Pan Size: 2 quart mold (or ramekin cups)
12 servings

2 c sugar
6-8 medium eggs, slightly beaten
1 qt half-and-half, warm
1 1/2 tsp vanilla
Brandy

Melt 1 c of the sugar over low heat. Do not stir. Remove from heat and sprinkle a few drops of brandy over hot sugar. Pour into mold and tilt to distribute over sides.

Whisk the other c of sugar into eggs and gradually add half-and-half.

Pour into mold and place into a pan of hot water. Bake 45 minutes or untill knife comes out clean when inserted in center. Cool completely and refrigerate.

 La Tourelle

2146 Monroe Avenue • 726.5771

Ooh-la-la! *White lace curtains, soft lighting with candles, sweet flowers. La Tourelle remains the oldest fine-dining restaurant in Memphis, and one of the most intimate and romantic. Owners Martha and Glenn Hays have employed some of the best chefs around, including Gene Bjorland, Erling Jensen, Justin Young and Cullen Kent. Chef Chris Dollar now has some big shoes to fill, and he is succeeding admirably. His amusette of Dijon and herb-crusted carpaccio of lamb loin with truffle oil and roasted tomato is a memorable treat. I inhaled the savory summer squash soup with curry! The gratin of lump crabmeat with artichokes was amazingly flavorful without seeming overly rich. Equally delicious—-the pompano en papillote served with jumbo lump crabmeat and saffron basmati pilaf. La Tourelle has received the DiRōNA award since 1993. Wine Spectator "Award of Excellence," 2004.*

LA TOURELLE SALAD

Mesclun greens (spring mix)
Tarragon aïoli
Spiced almonds
Thinly sliced Granny Smith (tart) apple, cored but not peeled

TARRAGON AÏOLI

2 tbsp minced shallots
1 clove peeled garlic
1 tbsp Dijon mustard
1 tbsp whole grain mustard
1 tsp white pepper
1 tsp salt
1/4 c chopped fresh tarragon
1/2 c tarragon vinegar
1 1/2 c olive oil

Purée shallots, garlic, mustards, salt, pepper and tarragon in food processor. While still mixing, drizzle in vinegar and olive oil.

SPICED ALMONDS

Whisk together 3 egg whites and 1/3 c of water. In separate bowl, mix together 3 tbsp chili powder, 1 tbsp habanera powder (or to taste), 3 tbsp sugar, 2 tbsp paprika and 2 tbsp salt. Toss 2 c sliced almonds in liquid and then in spices. Bake on a sheet pan at 350 for 3 or 4 minutes. Rotate almonds on sheet with spoon. Bake for 3 or 4 more minutes.

This makes a lot of almonds. Store in airtight container.

Mix the greens in the dressing. Place on separate salad plates. Sprinkle each salad with a few almonds and add 4 apples slices.

CASSIS ICE CREAM

(another old favorite)

8 c half-and-half
1 c sugar
1 1/2 tbsp vanilla
1 1/2 c cassis liqueur
1 18 oz jar black currant jam (or substitute blackberry seedless)

Mix all ingredients together. Pour into ice-cream maker and freeze.

Lolo's Table

128 Monroe • 522.9449

The new kid on the block is not so new any more. No question, Lolo's Table fits right into what could be called the best dining area in the city, downtown Memphis. Lolo's Low Country European cuisine is wonderfully flavorful. The slightly rustic surroundings are quaint and charming. Owners and staff are friendly and accommodating. Now let's get to the real meat here, and I don't mean steak—-although their Tuscan rib eye is something to write home about. I prefer the chicken scaloppini. Seriously savory. Chef Gary Hawkins is terrifically creative with salads. I recommend the "Shrimp Louis": mesclun, Gulf shrimp, grilled asparagus, petite tomatoes, and boiled egg, all tossed in rémoulade dressing (lunch menu only). Also, the crawfish potato salad (evening menu only): roasted corn, fingerling potatoes, and crawfish tails in a sherry Dijon vinaigrette.

SAUTÉED RED SNAPPER WITH PUTTANESCA

4 6 oz snapper filets
2 tbsp olive oil
1/4 c flour
Salt/pepper

1 yellow onion, small, julienned
1 tbsp capers, drained
2 anchovies, dried, minced
1/2 c Greek olives, pitted, roughly chopped
2 tsp garlic, chopped
1/2 tsp crushed red chiles
1/2 tsp oregano
1/2 tsp thyme
1/2 tsp basil
1 tbsp tomato paste
1 pound roma tomatoes, medium chopped (canned is fine)

Heat olive oil over medium heat in a saucepan, add onion, and cook 5 min. Add capers, anchovies, olives, garlic and herbs. Cook briefly to blend flavors. Add chopped tomatoes. Blend well. Add tomato paste. Check for salt and pepper. Let simmer over low heat 30-40 min.

When sauce is almost done, heat sauté pan over medium-high heat. Dry snapper filets, add salt and pepper, and then lightly dust in flour. When pan is hot, add fish, skin side up. Cook 3 min. till brown. Flip the fish over. Finish in oven 450, for 6-8 min. Pour sauce over snapper. Serve with rice pilaf and seasonal vegetable.

The puttanesca sauce goes well with pasta also.

WILD MUSHROOM BREAD PUDDING

2 tbsp olive oil
1/2 c shallots, chopped
1 pound mushrooms, sliced thin (shiitake, crimini, button)
1 tbsp garlic, chopped
2 tsp thyme
2 tsp oregano
Salt and pepper to taste
2 oz Madeira
3/4 c Gorgonzola
2 oz parsley, chopped
2 c heavy cream
1 c beef stock
4 eggs, large
4 egg whites
6 c bread, medium cubes, not too dry. Softer bread works well.

Heat olive oil in sauté pan over medium heat. Add shallots, cook 3-4 min. Add mushrooms, garlic, thyme and oregano. Cook 8-10 min. Add Madeira and reduce by half. Add Gorgonzola and parsley. Stir till cheese is blended in, check for salt and pepper. Let mixture cool.

For the custard, whip all ingredients together in a bowl, add the mushroom mixture and blend well. Add the cubed bread and let rest for 30 min. Pour mixture into baking dish with nonstick spray. Bake covered with foil for 30 min. Remove foil and bake 10-15 min longer.

Lulu Grill

565 Erin • 763.3677

Tucked away in a strip shopping center, this popular neighborhood bistro is sometimes overlooked. Lulu Grill serves consistently good American and international fare. I am a huge fan of Lulu's magnificent veal piccata. As a junior high school classmate of owner Leigh McLain, I am not surprised to find her running a highly successful restaurant with her husband, Don. Over the years, they have been fortunate to keep such an experienced staff, including Chef Scott DeLarme, a graduate of Johnson & Wales. Lulu Grill's award-winning desserts come from family recipes. Lulu's incredible coconut cake was featured in Memphis Magazine in September of 2003, as one of the "Top Ten Best Desserts" in the city. Lulu Grill is an excellent choice for Sunday brunch. Reasonably priced, and not too crowded.

Pan-Seared Venison Chop with Wild Mushroom Stuffing

Whole venison rack (or pre-cut chops)
Shiitake mushrooms
Oyster mushrooms
Celery
Yellow onion
Garlic
Breadcrumbs
Clarified butter
Thyme
Basil
Salt & pepper
Whole eggs

Cut venison rack into individual chops and make a pocket in each chop. Finely dice onion, celery and garlic. Slice mushrooms In a large pre-heated sauté pan, cook onions, celery and garlic for 1-2 minutes or until soft. Add mushrooms and seasonings and cook 2-3 minutes or until done. Place in a mixing bowl. Add eggs and breadcrumbs and adjust seasonings. Stuff venison chops and season with salt and pepper.

Pre-heat large sauté pan and sear chops on both sides Place pan in a 450 degree oven for 3-4 minutes (for medium rare). Plate and serve immediately.

Carrot Cake

1 3/4 c sugar
1 1/4 c Mazola Corn Oil
4 eggs
2 c cake flour
2 tsp baking powder
2 tsp baking soda
1 tsp salt
2 tsp cinnamon
3 c shredded carrots
1/2-3/4 c chopped nuts

Cream sugar – add oil slowly – add eggs one at a time. Sift flour, powder, salt and cinnamon together and add to first mixture. Fold in carrots and nuts. Bake in three 9" round greased and floured pans at 350 degrees for 20-25 minutes.

Icing
3 oz soft cream cheese
1/4 c butter
1 tsp vanilla
1 1/2-2 1/2 c powdered sugar (sifted)

Beat cream cheese, butter and vanilla – slowly add powdered sugar. Frost layers and top and add a handful of nuts on top.

McEwen's On Monroe

122 Monroe Avenue • 527.7085

Being one of the first on the block, McEwen's On Monroe, serving Southern Fusion cuisine, has not lost its charm. Just a little more seasoned. Foodies continue to buzz over this dining destination. A wide assortment of interesting, creative entrees, appetizers and salads to choose from. Portions are ample. The sublime sweet potato-crusted catfish, served with Creole honey mustard and macaroni and cheese, is very popular. Menu changes quarterly. Big selection of wines. Casual and comfortable. Call ahead for reservations.

Sweet Potato Encrusted Catfish

Ingredients:

Catfish filleted, 7 to 9 oz
Sweet potato (peeled and shredded)
1 egg
2 oz of milk
1/2 oz olive oil
1/4 tsp of butter

Sauté pan 12" in diameter.

Begin by combining the egg and milk in a small bowl with a whisk. Reserve for later use. Using a cheese grater, peel and shred the sweet potato. Reserve for later use. Lay your catfish flesh side up. Using a pastry brush, lightly brush the egg wash over the fish. Firmly press the shredded sweet potatoes over the catfish making sure to cover the entire fillet. In your 12" sauté pan, heat the olive oil and add the butter till almost the point of smoking. Add your catfish sweet potato side down. Cook till the edges of the catfish start to brown. Flip the catfish over ever so lightly, making sure not to burn yourself with the oil. Add the catfish to a preheated 350 degree oven for 6 minutes or until a desired doneness.

Green Corn Pudding

This dish is served at McEwen's on Monroe as a side dish with the beef tenderloin, but could be served with damn near anything you want. Good for any dining occasion.

Ingredients:
6 ears of fresh corn
4 strips of bacon julienned or diced
1 c small diced onion
1 medium sized green bell pepper, diced
1 medium sized red bell pepper, diced
1 jalapeño, diced
8 eggs
1 qt of heavy cream
1/2 qt of half-and-half
1 oz Tabasco sauce
1 oz Worcestershire sauce
1/2 tsp nutmeg
1 oz fresh chopped thyme
1 oz fresh chopped basil
1/4 c fresh chopped parsley

In a sauté pan, render the bacon (sauté the bacon and then remove the fat.) Add the peppers and onion and begin sautéing. When cooked to desired doneness, reserve in a mixing bowl and cool. Once cooled, add the cream, half-and-half and the eggs. Having once roasted the ears of corn, shuck and slice along the edges, getting your kernels. Mix all ingredients in the mixing bowl, adding salt and pepper to taste. Grease a casserole dish. Add your corn pudding combination to the casserole dish. Place into a 300 degree oven for 40 minutes. Reserve until service.

The term "green corn" comes from an old Southern term meaning fresh from the field.

Paulette's

2110 Madison Avenue • 726.5128

Step into a little bit of France, or should we say Hungary, Belgium, or Holland. With its European flavor, this fine-dining establishment is frequented by locals and tourists alike. Paulette's has been honored in Memphis Magazine in more categories than any other restaurant. The menu offers a variety of steaks, seafood, chicken, crepes, salads and soups. And although Paulette's is not a steak house, I would put its filet mignon up against that of any steak house in Memphis. Portions are generous, and consistency reigns. Desserts are heavenly. The "Kahlua-Mocha Parfait Pie" ("K-Pie," for short) is my favorite. There is nothing like it!

YELLOW SQUASH SOUP

3-3 1/2 pounds yellow squash, diced
3 c diced onion
1 c finely diced celery
1/4 c diced carrots
4 tbsp butter
2 tsp dried basil
1 1/4 qts chicken broth
1 pt half-and-half
1 c heavy cream
1/4 tsp ground cloves
1/4 tsp nutmeg
1/2 tsp white pepper
1 tsp salt
1/2 tsp sugar

Cook vegetables in basil and butter about 10 minutes, stirring constantly. Add chicken broth, then cover and bring to boil. Simmer until vegetables are tender. Purée mixture in a blender, then return to the pot and add half-and-half and heavy cream. Heat but do not boil. Add remaining seasonings and stir well. Garnish with a dash of nutmeg in the center of the soup.

This soup can be served hot or cold.

Serves 6 to 8.

FILET PAULETTE

8 (4 oz) beef tenderloin filets
Cracked black pepper to taste
1/2 c butter
1 onion, julienned
1 bell pepper, julienned
2 c heavy cream
1/2 c dry white wine
1/4 c Worcestershire sauce
4 tsp lemon juice
1 tomato, julienned
4 tomato wedges
4 sprigs of parsley

Encrust tenderloin medallions with cracked pepper. Sauté in hot butter to desired doneness then remove. In the same pan, sauté onion and bell pepper in the pepper-butter sauce (add more butter if necessary) until tender. Add cream along with wine, Worcestershire, and a dash of lemon juice. Return meat to pan and cook on high flame until cream sauce boils; add julienned tomato. Remove and arrange vegetables on top of meat, then pour cream sauce over all. Garnish tomatoes wedges and parsley.

Serves 4.

Stella

39 South Main Street • 526.4950

The old Brodnax Jewelers, formerly at the corner of Main and Monroe, offered us fabulous jewels. Now Stella, located in the old Brodnax Building, is itself a gem. Chef Johnny Kirk, who has worked under some well-known chefs, is now making a name for himself. The James Beard Foundation named Chef Kirk "A Rising Star in American Cuisine" in June of 2005. His menu is quite strong. Fish entrées include wild Atlantic salmon, served with ricotta gnocchi, summer squash, carrots, asparagus, and chanterelle mushrooms, in orange and brown butter sauce; and trout amandine, made with farm-raised North Carolina trout, lump crabmeat, charred tomato, and sweet pea couscous. For diners who choose beef, there's prime filet mignon with chilled fingerling potato and applewood smoked bacon salad, Madeira demi-glace, and smoked tomato aïoli. Extremely popular, Stella is a sure place to see and be seen.

CRAWFISH CHEESECAKE

12 oz cream cheese
4 whole eggs
12 oz mascarpone cheese
1 egg yolk
2 c crawfish - chopped
1 tbsp flour
1 tbsp sherry
1 tbsp sugar
1 tsp cumin
Salt
1 tbsp creole seasoning
White pepper
1/4 lemon, juiced

Cream the cream cheese Add all other ingredients and fold together. Pour into crust. Bake 15 minutes at 475 in a 10" round spring form pan. Continue cooking for 2 hours at 300 degrees (check after 1 1/2 hours) Serves 8.

 Tsunami

928 South Cooper • 274.2556

Looking for an upscale place to go for some highly imaginative, creative eats? At Tsunami, Chef Ben Smith seems to be catching up with his extremely talented father, multi-media artist Dolph Smith. The difference is that Chef Smith exercises his artistry in food. His Pacific Rim cuisine, made with the freshest ingredients, is a spicy addition to the Memphis restaurant scene. A trusted destination in Cooper-Young, Tsunami remains an anchor in the area. The energy at Tsunami is exciting. The "small plates" are a hit, for those who enjoy sampling various menu items. For diners who prefer larger portions, the main menu offers steamed mussels in Thai red curry sauce, for instance, and black bean soup with smoked chili cream. Although the roasted sea bass on black Thai rice is excellent, I would go to bat every day for the "Hot and Pungent Shrimp in Coconut Milk." Chef Smith's own crème brûlée was featured on the cover of Memphis Magazine in September 2003, as one of the "Ten Best Desserts in Memphis." Memphis Magazine's "Restaurant Guide" for 2005 recognized Tsunami as "#1 Seafood Restaurant in Memphis."

Chilled Avocado Soup

Juice of 2 limes
Juice of 1 lemon
8 ripe avocados
16 oz plain non-fat yogurt
2 c milk
2 c vegetable or chicken stock
1 tsp ground cumin
1 small red onion, diced
Salt to taste

Peel and seed the avocados and toss them together in a large bowl with the lemon juice, lime juice and yogurt. Puree the mixture in a blender or food processor until smooth. Add remaining ingredients and chill well before serving. Serves 6.

Grand Marnier Soufflé

(makes 4)

2 oz unsalted butter
4 oz flour
13 oz milk
5 egg yolks
4 oz Grand Marnier
3 egg whites
6 oz sugar

In heavy saucepan melt butter add flour and mix well. Add milk and stir until all lumps are gone. Remove from heat. Stir egg yolks into flour mixture one at a time. Slowly fold in Grand Marnier. Beat egg whites to soft peaks, slowly add sugar with machine running and continue beating to stiff peaks. Fold egg whites into roux mixture. Portion evenly into four large soufflé dishes that have been buttered and sugared and bake at 400 degrees for 30 minutes. Sprinkle with powdered sugar and serve immediately.

Wally Joe Restaurant

5040 Sanderlin, Suite 105 • 818.0821

Posh it is. The design of Wally Joe Restaurant is the work of the award-winning Askew Nixon Ferguson Architects, Inc. The atmosphere is elegant, cosmopolitan, and no-nonsense. Chef Wally Joe serves Modern American cuisine with French and Asian influences. He and his staff are committed to working with farmers and fishermen who share his philosophy of offering only the best. The menu is sophisticated and original. Among the unusual appetizers, there's Hudson Valley foie gras seared with steel-cut oatmeal, roasted local peaches, and cinnamon honey gastrique. The attention-getting list of entrees includes Sonoma Pacific Pastures veal with truffle cheese polenta, sweetbreads, oyster mushrooms, boccolini, and natural jus. Pastry Chef Jorge Noriega makes knock-out desserts, such as the incredible roasted blueberry tart with brown butter ice cream and blueberry-huckleberry gastrique. The French press coffee, prepared individually, is a nice touch. Wally Joe's is centrally located on Sanderlin, across from The Racquet Club. Menu changes seasonally.

Grilled Loin of Lamb with Black Olive Crust, Celeriac-Potato Hash & Oven-Dried Tomato Red Wine Sauce

Serves 4

2 boneless lamb loins, trimmed of fat and silver skin
1 c black olives, dried in the oven for 3 hours at the lowest temperature (200 degrees)
2 tbsp Dijon mustard
1/2 c breadcrumbs
1 medium celeriac, shredded
1 small onion, julienned
1/2 c heavy cream
1 tbsp all-purpose flour
1 tbsp chopped garlic
8 oven dried tomatoes, chopped
1 shallot, chopped
2 c dry red wine
1/2 c balsamic vinegar
1 tbsp granulated sugar
1 c veal stock

Place black olives on a sheet pan and dry in the oven at the lowest temperature for 3 hours. Pulverize in a food processor or chop fine with a knife. Mix with the breadcrumbs. Reserve.

In a mixing bowl, combine the shredded potatoes, celeriac, onions, garlic, cream and flour. Mix well and season with salt and pepper. Divide the mixture into 4 equal portions.

In a sauté pan with olive oil, fry the celeriac-potato hashes until browned on both sides. Reserve.

Sweat the shallots with the tomatoes in a saucepan, add the red wine and reduce down to 1/2 c. Add the vinegar and sugar and reduce again by half. Add the veal stock and reduce to sauce consistency. Season to taste with salt and pepper.

Season the lamb loins with salt and pepper. Sear in a hot sauté pan with a touch of olive oil on both sides. Remove from the pan and wipe off excess oil. Brush one side of the lamb loins with the mustard and coat with the black olive crust mix.

Finish in a preheated 450 degree oven for 7 minutes for medium rare, or longer if desired.

After the lamb has rested for 4 minutes, slice each loin into 6 equal slices.

Place a hash in the center of a dinner plate, top with 3 slices of lamb, and ladle sauce around the lamb and hash.

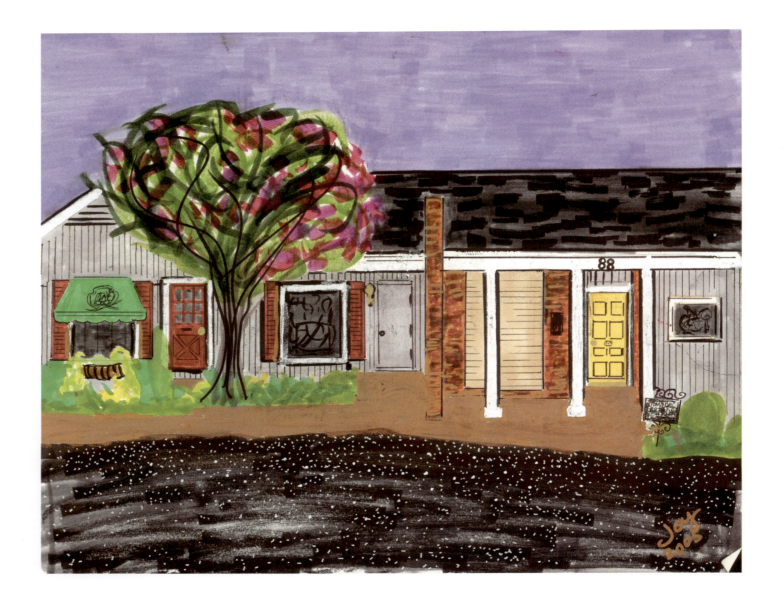

Woman's Exchange Tea Room

88 Racine • 327.5681

As a little girl back in the 1960's, I remember going to The Woman's Exchange of Memphis with my mother, and enjoying the chicken salad sandwiches, milk and fancy cookies. Today, not much has changed. Sure, the dining area has been enlarged and redecorated, and business is computerized, but the food remains the same, and that is a good thing. One could honestly say the food is "just like my grandmother used to make." Menu changes daily, with standards like "Seafood Charleston," chicken Tetrazzini, corn chowder, quiche Lorraine and purple hull peas, offered on a rotating basis. Every Thursday, though, regular Woman's Exchange diners know to expect Chef Emanuel Bailey (known as "Rev") to be serving his fantastic beef tenderloin. Lunch only, Monday through Friday. Make time to shop for unique gift items and exquisite, handmade children's clothing. In November and December, the impressive Christmas Shop is open.

SEAFOOD BISQUE

10 tbsp butter
1/2 c flour
2 c clams, minced
1 c half-and-half
1/2 bunch green onions
4 c milk
1/2 clove garlic, minced
1 pound crab meat
1/2 pound shelled shrimp, cooked and diced
1/2 c dry white table wine
2 3/4 tbsp dry sherry

Melt 1/2 c butter in large saucepan. Blend in flour and cook 2 minutes. Drain liquid from clams. Put clams aside. Stir liquid into butter and flour mixture. Stir until blended. Slowly stir in milk and half-and-half, and cook until soup is thickened. Chop onions finely and sauté them in a large skillet. Add garlic and remaining butter. Add the crab, shrimp, drained clams, and cook in the butter mixture, stirring until seafood is heated thoroughly. Do not boil. Add seafood mixture to soup mixture – add wine and sherry – heat to serving temperature. Another suggestion would be to add the wine to the bisque as directed, but serve the sherry in a small container on the side. Each person could add the amount desired. Serves 8.

You asked for it! Substitute margarine, skim milk and skimmed evaporated milk for the half-and-half.

CARAMEL BROWNIES

2 c light brown sugar
1 stick butter, softened
2 eggs
1 3/4 c flour
1 tsp baking powder
1 tsp vanilla
1/4 tsp salt
1 c pecans, chopped

Preheat oven to 325. Blend softened butter and sugar; add eggs, beat well. Add remaining ingredients and mix. Pour into greased 8x10 pan; bake in 325 oven for 30 minutes. Makes 16. Serve with Brown Sugar Icing.

BROWN SUGAR ICING

3/4 c light brown sugar
2/3 c white sugar , granulated
2 1/4 tsp dark Karo syrup
1/2 c heavy cream
1/4 c butter

Mix all ingredients together and bring to a boil. Cook for 15-20 min. to a soft ball stage (230 on a candy thermometer). Stir several times. Pour over cool caramel brownies. Allow to cool before cutting. Covers one pan of brownies

Some fare to be recognized that is absolutely tonic

from restaurants that are not featured in this book.

All of which I could eat over and over and over again.

AT THE LITTLE TEA SHOP ON MONROE-- "BROCCOLI PUFFS": A CASSEROLE OF BROCCOLI, CHEESE AND RICE (SERVED THURSDAY ONLY); AND THEIR MELT-IN-YOUR-MOUTH CORNBREAD, FEATURED IN GOURMET MAGAZINE, JULY 2005

FROM PETE & SAM'S RESTAURANT ON PARK--
SAUSAGE PIZZA MADE WITH PETE & SAM'S OWN SAUSAGE AND TOMATO SAUCE, ON A LIGHT, THIN CRUST

FROM CAFÉ DE FRANCE INSIDE PALLADIO MALL ON CENTRAL-- SMOKED PORK LOIN WITH MANGO HORSERADISH MAYONNAISE AND MANCHEGO CHEESE ON CIABATTA

AT AMERIGO ON RIDGEWAY--
CHICKEN MARSALA: SAUTEED CHICKEN BREAST, MARSALA WINE BROWN SAUCE, MUSHROOMS AND ARTICHOKES

FROM THE HALF SHELL ON MENDENHALL- SEAFOOD GUMBO MADE WITH FRESH VEGETABLES, CAJUN SAUSAGE, GULF SHRIMP, AND CRAWFISH TAILS, THICKENED WITH A RICH, DARK ROUX

AT MORTIMER'S RESTAURANT ON NORTH PERKINS-- FRIED SHRIMP: JUMBO GULF SHRIMP BREADED BY HAND AND DEEP FRIED

FROM SALSA MEXICAN RESTAURANT ON POPLAR--
TORTILLA SOUP WITH CHICKEN: A MEXICAN VEGETABLE SOUP WITH CHICKEN

Thoughts on Food

Every joy is beyond all others. The fruit we are eating is always the best fruit of all. C.S. Lewis

Fish, to taste right, must swim three times — in water, in butter and in wine. Polish Proverb

When I am in really great trouble, as anyone who knows me intimately will tell you, I refuse everything except food and drink. Oscar Wilde

Strange to see how a good dinner and feasting reconciles everybody. Samuel Pepys

We could not have had a better dinner, had there been a Synod of Cooks. Samuel Johnson

The French cook, we open tins. John Galsworthy

The meek shall eat and be satisfied: They shall praise the Lord that seek him: Your heart shall live forever. Psalm 22:26

The only emperor is the emperor of ice cream. Wallace Stevens

There is no sincerer love than the love of food. George Bernard Shaw

Our lives are not in the laps of the gods, but in the laps of our cooks. Lin Yutang

PHOTO BY LARRY KUZNIEWSKI

Joy Bateman IS A NATIVE MEMPHIAN. SHE HAS THREE CHILDREN, WILLIAM C. BATEMAN III, BROWN BURCH AND ANNA WUNDERLICH; PLUS SON-IN-LAW BENJAMIN AND A GRANDCHILD ON THE WAY. IN ADDITION TO PURSUING HER INTERESTS IN ART AND RESTAURANT DINING, THE AUTHOR LIKES TO COOK FOR HER FAMILY AND FRIENDS, PLAY TENNIS AND SPEND TIME AT THE BEACH. SHE IS PRESENTLY EMPLOYED BY *MEMPHIS MAGAZINE* AS SENIOR ACCOUNT EXECUTIVE. PREVIOUSLY, JOY WORKED FOR 17 YEARS AT *MEMPHIS BUSINESS JOURNAL*, WHERE SHE WON NUMEROUS AWARDS FOR OUTSTANDING SALES. JOY IS A CURRENT MEMBER OF ST. ANDREWS PRESBYTERIAN CHURCH, KIWANIS INTERNATIONAL, AND THE AMERICAN CULINARY FEDERATION.